KNOWLEDGE ENCYCLOPEDIA
MISSION EXPLORATION
SPACE

© Wonder House Books 2022

All rights reserved. No part of this book may be reproduced or transmitted in any form by any means, electronic or mechanical, including photocopying and recording, or by any information storage and retrieval system except as may be expressly permitted in writing by the publisher.

(An imprint of Prakash Books)

contact@wonderhousebooks.com

Disclaimer: The information contained in this encyclopedia has been collated with inputs from subject experts. All information contained herein is true to the best of the Publisher's knowledge. Maps are only indicative in nature.

ISBN : 9789390391660

Table of Contents

Exploring Space	3
A Brief History	4–5
The Cold War and Space Race	6–7
The First Space Explorers	8–9
The American Space Programme	10–11
The Soviet Space Programme	12–13
All about Astronauts	14–15
The First Humans in Space	16
The First Americans in Space	17
The First Human Beings to Reach the Moon	18
Extravehicular Activity or Spacewalks	19
Milestones in Space Exploration	20–21
The Apollo Programme (1963–1972)	22–23
Mission Highlights of the Apollo Flights	24–25
Jupiter and the Juno Mission	26–27
Exploring the Red Planet	28–29
Challenges and Issues in Space Exploration	30–31
Word Check	32

EXPLORING SPACE

The human race has been curious about outer space and celestial bodies for a long, long time. This interest in the unknown and the curiosity to explore new worlds and frontiers has been an enduring one. It has encouraged human beings to push the boundaries of science and technology, and has challenged us beyond imagination. More than 400 years ago, astronomers had to rely only on their eyes to observe the skies, but with the advent of the telescope and, much later, rockets and spacecrafts, they were able to delve deeper into the mysteries of outer space. Space exploration has thus, reaped multiple benefits for humanity for decades, including a deeper understanding of our universe, and particularly, the solar system. It has unravelled answers to basic questions like the place of humans and Earth in the vast cosmos, and the history of our planetary system.

▼ *A rocket blasting off from Earth*

A Brief History

By the early 20th century, rocket technology had progressed to a point where it was possible to send objects with sufficient speeds to orbit Earth and perhaps even escape Earth's gravity to go further. The idea of human space exploration gained popularity amongst the public, and even scientific and military planners started to initiate space projects and develop launch vehicles.

★ Early Rocket Pioneers in the 1900s

A Russian school teacher and mathematician, Konstantin Tsiolkovsky was one of the first persons to study the use of rockets for spaceflight in the 1900s. His article, *Exploration of Cosmic Space by Means of Reaction Devices,* in 1903, mentioned several principles of spaceflight. His work influenced rocket research in the Soviet Union and Europe.

In the United States of America, Robert Goddard was inspired by space exploration after reading H.G. Wells's book, *The War of the Worlds*. He was awarded his first two patents for rocket technology in 1914. When Goddard claimed that rockets could be used to send objects to the Moon, he was ridiculed, after which he did most of his work in secrecy. As a physics professor, Goddard experimented with liquid-fuelled rockets and built engines and more advanced rockets.

Hermann Oberth's books and work explained the mathematics behind the theory of rocketry, rocket design, the idea of constructing space stations and outer space journeys to other planets. *Ways to Spaceflight* was his second significant book. Inspired by his work, rocket clubs and associations—including the Verein für Raumschiffahrt (VfR: Society for Spaceship Travel)—were set up in Germany. These groups attempted to put Oberth's ideas into practice.

▲ *A theoretical scientist and a practical engineer, Dr Robert H. Goddard (1882–1945) is acknowledged as the father of American rocketry*

★ Other Pioneers

Frenchman Robert Esnault-Pelterie wrote about the theoretical features of spaceflight in 1907, and Austrian Eugen Sänger suggested developing a 'rocket plane' that would reach speeds of 10,000 kilometres per hour and achieve a height of 65 kilometres.

Incredible Individuals

At 20, German-born Wernher von Braun (1912–1977) became the chief engineer of a rocket-development team for the German army. In 1933 Nazi Germany, Braun was titled the civilian head of that team. He played a significant role in all areas of rocket science and space exploration, first in Germany, and after World War II, in the USA. Through his talks and writings, Braun helped popularise the concept of human space travel and created an open environment for government space activities.

▶ *A key figure in America's space programme, Wernher von Braun standing near the F-1 engines of the Saturn V Dynamic Test Vehicle, at the US Space and Rocket Center in Alabama*

Rockets: Early Development

Germany

Influenced by the rocket-building activity of the VfR in the 1930s, the German military started making rockets at a centre close to the Baltic Sea. The V-2 ballistic missile was developed and launched there in 1942. Initially used as a military weapon, it later served as a prototype in the American and Russian space programmes. After World War II, some of the Germans surrendered to the USA and went there along with the engineering plans and parts required to build V-2s. Amongst them was Wernher von Braun, who played a crucial role in early rocket development in both Germany and America.

▲ *Wernher von Braun (seen in the picture in a black suit)*

United States

In the 1930s, young American engineers under the leadership of Frank Malina worked on rocket science. Aerodynamicist Theodore von Kármán and Chinese engineer Qian Xuesen supported them. Xuesen went back to China in the 1950s and pioneered rocketry. In 1943, Malina and his colleagues developed weapons which were modified for use in early space experiments in the USA. From 1946 till 1951, several experiments were conducted by US scientists on captured V-2 rockets. The Upper Atmosphere Research Panel headed by physicist James Van Allen worked on the scientific uses of rocket launches.

▲ *(From L-R): William Pickering, James Van Allen and Wernher von Braun—the brains behind Explorer 1 (1958); Physicist James van Allen seen at the Smithsonian National Air and Space Museum in Washington D.C., USA; American engineer Frank Malina at the White Sands Missile Range, seen with the fifth WAC Corporal. In 1943, Malina and his colleagues called their group the Jet Propulsion Laboratory, which became a centre for missile research and development in USA*

Soviet Union

In 1921, the Russian government built a military centre focused on rocket research. In the 1930s, Valentin Glushko did groundbreaking work on rocket engines. In 1933, members of GIRD (Group for the Study of Reactive Motion) were responsible for launching the first Soviet rocket that worked on liquid fuel.

▶ *A stamp commemorating Valentin Glushko*

The Cold War and Space Race

Both the Cold War and the Space Race were important and exciting events in the history of space exploration. Read on to find out more.

The Cold War

After World War II, from 1947 to 1991, the USA and the Soviet Union—the then most powerful nations in the world—were embroiled in a 'Cold War' i.e., a war in which there was no direct battle, minimal use of weapons and both parties were not officially in a state of war. Both countries had different political ideologies; while USA was a capitalist democracy, the Soviet Union was a Communist totalitarian regime. The countries were motivated by both ideological and geopolitical factors. While both had acquired atomic bombs, it would have been disastrous for them to engage in a real war. So, they competed on other fronts in a race for supremacy. Space was one such front.

What was the Space Race?

Both the USA and the Soviet Union tried their best to gain expertise in space exploration, space flights and rocket technology. This resulted in the Space Race. The rivalry between the two nations was so great that both had secret satellites which they used to spy over each other's activities. Military usage to locate an enemy was one of the main aims of spaceflight.

▲ *The Space Race ultimately became a race to reach the Moon first*

Publicity Versus Secrecy

The Space Race also showed philosophical differences between the two nations in the way they functioned. Military and civilian agencies were separate in the USA. Only military space missions were kept confidential. Civilian space activities were widely publicised, especially the race to the Moon.

On the other hand, all the space programmes in the Soviet Union were run very secretively, and as part of the military. No prior publicity was done regarding their launches, and only those missions which were successful were made public.

Since the Soviet Union was so silent and secretive about their space activities, the leaders of the USA feared a nuclear attack and wanted to know what their rival was doing. So, they took photographs of the Soviet Union from space from 1960 to 1972 as part of a military observation project named Corona.

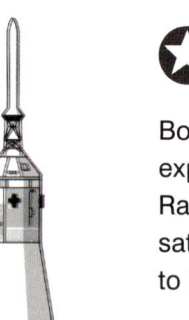

◀ *The American Saturn V rocket aided NASA's Apollo programme in the human exploration of the Moon*

Incredible Individuals

Russian scientist Sergey Pavlovich Korolyov (1907–1966) was best known as the 'Chief Designer', having played a key role in the design, testing and construction of the Soviet Union's guided missiles, rockets, and spacecrafts (including Vostok, Voskhod, Soyuz and several others).

The Moscow Group for the Study of Reactive Motion was formed by Korolyov along with F.A. Tsander. In 1933, this group was responsible for launching Russia's first liquid-propellant rocket. After World War II, amongst other things, Korolyov improved the German V-2 missile, increasing its range to about 685 kilometres. His work on developing a series of ballistic missiles in 1953 resulted in Russia's first intercontinental ballistic missile (ICBM).

Korolyov was the guiding force behind the Soviet Union's space flight programme.

SPACE | MISSION EXPLORATION

⭐ Race to the Moon

At the beginning of the Space Race, there were no clear goals, nor were there any defined rules. At first, the Soviet Union led with the launch of Sputnik 1, the world's first artificial satellite. Their achievements included putting the first living creature, Laika the dog in space; the first man, Yuri Gagarin in space; the first woman, Valentina Tereshkova in space; the first spacewalk, etc.

The pressure to catch up inspired the US. President John F Kennedy's declaration in 1961, "I believe that this nation should commit itself to achieving the goal before this decade is out, of landing a man on the Moon and returning him safely to the Earth," reflected USA's resolve of landing a man on the Moon.

This marked a turning point in the Space Race—which turned into a race to be the first on the Moon.

While the Americans were open about their goal, the Soviets, for many years, were very secretive and even denied their participation in the race to the Moon.

▲ US President John F Kennedy addressing a crowd of 35,000 people at Rice University in 1962, where he said, "But I do say space can be explored and mastered without feeding the fires of war…" and also referred to America's Moon mission

◀ Artificial satellites in space have multiple uses: they help in predicting the weather, in communications and taking photographs of celestial objects, which help scientists gain a better understanding of our universe, including the solar system

💡 Isn't It Amazing!

Explorer 1 was the first space satellite put into space by NASA in 1958, and was responsible for discovering the innermost regions of the Van Allen radiation belts—two regions of charged particles surrounding our planet. This made history since it was the first scientific discovery to be made by a man-made (artificial) satellite.

▶ The Explorer 1 space satellite just before its launch at NASA's Jet Propulsion Lab

The First Space Explorers

The Soviet Union initially led the Space Race by sending the first living creature and the first man into space. However, the USA won by becoming the first country to send a human being to the Moon. Let us see who these first and early space explorers were.

⭐ Soviet Union: Racing Ahead

The world's first artificial satellite, Sputnik 1, launched by the Soviet Union on October 4, 1957, marked the beginning of the Space Age. It weighed 83.6 kilograms, and circled Earth every 96 minutes until early 1958, after which it fell back and burned up in Earth's atmosphere.

One month later, Sputnik 2 carried Laika, a dog, into space. Similar experiments were carried out on different animals via eight other Sputnik missions to test the spacecrafts' life-support systems and re-entry procedures. These helped collect vital information about the temperatures, pressure, particles, radiation and magnetic fields in space.

In hot pursuit, USA launched their satellite Explorer I in January 1958.

▲ A model of Sputnik 1

◀ America's answer to the Soviet Union's Sputnik—Explorer 1

⭐ Soviet Cosmonauts

While 'astronaut' refers to a person from USA, Europe, Canada or Japan, who is certified and trained to travel in space, 'cosmonaut' is a term used in Russia and the former Soviet Union for a person certified by the Russian Space Agency to work in space. On April 12, 1961, the Soviet Union sent the first cosmonaut, Yuri Gagarin into space aboard the Vostok I. Over the next two years, there were six Vostok space missions. Except for the first two, all the other Vostok spacecrafts went up in pairs. Each of them bettered the time in orbit and distance covered. In June 1963, Vostok 6 transported the first female cosmonaut, Valentina Tereshkova into space. The Vostok spacecrafts travelled extremely close together (sometimes as close as 4.8 kilometres). This paved the way for future space dockings between orbiting vehicles.

American Astronauts

A few weeks after the Vostok 1 launch, the United States began the Mercury mission—a series of manned spaceflights. Alan B. Shepard Jr. was the first American in space and undertook a 15-minute flight aboard Freedom 7. One year later, astronaut John H. Glenn became the first American to orbit Earth. In May 1963, Faith 7 was the final flight in the Mercury series, and the first US spaceflight that lasted more than a day, orbiting Earth 22 times.

▶ *The Mercury Seven astronauts posing in front of an F-106 Delta Dart*

The US Moon Mission

Apollo 11 was the historic mission that took the first human beings to the Moon. It was launched on July 16, 1969 and successfully returned to Earth on July 24. The astronauts aboard, Neil Armstrong, Buzz Aldrin (real name Edwin Eugene Aldrin Jr.) and Michael Collins undertook various tasks to collect important information after arriving on the lunar surface, including measuring the composition of the solar wind reaching the Moon, setting up devices to figure out the precise distance between Earth and the Moon, and measuring **moonquakes** and the impact of meteors. They also collected rock and soil samples from the Moon's surface.

▼ *Vostok 1—the Soviet spacecraft that took the first human to space*

Incredible Individuals

Katherine Johnson, an American mathematician, was a genius. She was amongst the first three African Americans who got selected for a graduate programme at West Virginia University. Johnson was responsible for calculating and analysing the flight paths of several spacecrafts, including the path for Freedom 7. She played a key role in most of the important NASA space programmes for more than 30 years. She was a key team member of the Apollo 11 mission.

▲ *Katherine Johnson after receiving the Presidential Medal of Freedom in November 2015*

The American Space Programme

One of the main reasons why the US space programme started was to invent larger rockets for military warfare and national defence. Since then, it has grown by leaps and bounds and has accomplished things that make not just Americans, but all of humanity proud.

⭐ The Beginning

The American space programme emerged as a result of the intermediate range and intercontinental ballistic missile programmes (IRBM and ICBM). These were started after World War II by the US military in order to launch larger warheads into space with the help of rockets.

In the 1950s, the US government's priority was to develop the Utility-2 (U-2) aircraft to conduct military observations of the Soviet Union. In 1960, when a U-2 was shot down, Americans realised that the only way to 'observe' the Soviet Union was through satellites and space exploration.

While the US was capable of sending a satellite into Earth's orbit by the mid-1950s, they believed a 'space race' was unnecessary. The Soviet Union beat them to it when they launched Sputnik in 1957. After several failed attempts, it took America another year and a half before they could successfully launch Explorer 1 and later, Vanguard.

⭐ The Birth of NASA

The National Aeronautics and Space Administration (NASA) was established in 1958 in response to the Soviet launching of Sputnik. NASA's mission was to conduct research, develop vehicles and undertake space exploration activities within and outside Earth's atmosphere.

The following four directorates help NASA carry out its many functions:

- **Aeronautics** (the science of designing, building, and operating an aircraft) Research for developing cutting-edge aviation technologies;
- Science: programmes to understand the origin, structure and evolution of the universe, the solar system and Earth;
- Space Technology: Expansion of space science and exploration technologies;
- Human Exploration and Operations: Managing manned space missions, operations for launch services and space transportation and communications for manned and robotic space exploration programmes.

The Congress had established the National Advisory Committee for Aeronautics (NACA) in 1915. NASA was an off-shoot of the same.

SPACE | MISSION EXPLORATION

◀ NASA's John F Kennedy Space Center in Florida, USA

⭐ Major Achievements

By the early years of President Kennedy's administration, NASA was fairly well-established and gained momentum when he committed to send an American to the Moon. Thus began NASA's legendary Apollo missions which enabled Armstrong to be the first man to land on the Moon in 1969. NASA undertook several other unmanned missions to explore the solar system, including Viking, Mariner, Voyager and Galileo.

NASA also launched several satellites, including the Landsat satellite series to collect data on Earth's features and natural resources, and other weather and communications satellites.

The **space shuttle**, the world's first reusable spacecraft designed by NASA took off on its first flight in April 1981 and went on 135 flights before its mission ended in 2011. A space shuttle is a partially reusable rocket-launched vehicle, which transports astronauts and cargo to and from spacecrafts that are orbiting in space, and one that is capable of landing on a runway when it comes back to Earth.

◀ The NASA-built space shuttle was the first spacecraft in history that had the ability to carry large satellites to and from orbit

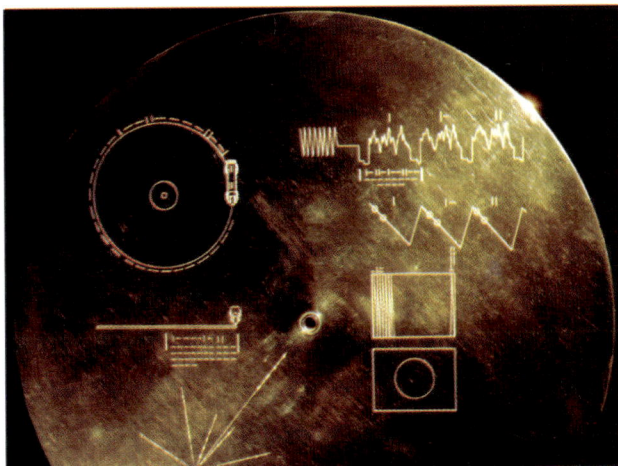

◀ One of the two copies of the Voyager Golden Record

💡 Isn't It Amazing!

NASA's spacecraft Voyager 1, launched in 1977, is orbiting in **interstellar space** since 2012, and it will be the first man-made object to leave the solar system once it passes the Oort Cloud, after a few hundred years. No other spacecraft in the world has travelled so far.

Voyager 1 has on-board one copy of the 'Golden Record'—a message from the human race to the universe, which comprises greetings in 55 different languages, photographs of people and places on Earth and a wide range of music from Beethoven to Chuck Berry!

The Soviet Space Programme

The Soviet Union's space programme was divided into two parts—military and scientific. All their military missions were well-guarded secrets. Only some aspects of their space programme were publicised.

★ Initial Development

The launch of the first satellite took the world by storm and inspired others to make advances in space. The satellite was named Sputnik, which in Russian means 'fellow traveller'.

At first the Soviets' intent was to be seen as a leader in technical, scientific and military power. In the 1960s, however, they expanded their goal and launched new satellites for the purpose of military and commercial use.

Satellites for **meteorology** and civil communication were publicised, but those designed for photographic and military observation through Electronic Intelligence Satellites (ELINT), radar calibration, secret communication, navigation and the study of **geodesy** and satellite interception were disguised as part of their scientific research. The actual objective was mostly military use.

★ Shift in Focus

In the latter half of the 1960s, the Soviet Union attempted to test bigger and more intricate **rocket boosters** and space vehicles. But they were not completely successful and were not able to develop a booster which was big enough for a human mission to the Moon. Since the USA was already ahead of them with their Apollo project, the Soviets began to focus their human space programme on space stations in orbit around Earth instead. A space station is an artificial structure placed in space and has a pressurised enclosure, power, supplies and environmental systems to support human habitation for a long duration. This shift in focus contributed greatly to inventions in space, as space stations have come a long way since then, and now form an integral part of the space framework.

◀ *The Soviet Union's Soyuz rocket being launched*

▲ *Russia's Soyuz Spacecraft*

Military Goals

In the early 1970s, they largely focused on building advanced and improved space systems for supporting the military. They also attempted to maintain their image of being experts in space exploration by advertising about the Salyut space stations. Salyut 1 was their first space station launched into orbit in 1971, with its three-person crew that spent 23 days on-board. Unfortunately, they didn't survive their journey back to Earth. Salyut 2 was also not successful and exploded after it reached orbit. Salyut 3 and 5 were military space stations, while 4, 6 and 7 were for scientific research.

The Soviet Union's space programme was largely focused on military efforts, with nearly 70 per cent of its annual launches being for this purpose. In the 1960s, the joint military-cum-civil missions had increased, but not significantly. The USA, however, had a more even distribution between military and non-military initiatives.

In Real Life

Launched in 1977 and 1982 respectively, the Salyut 6 and 7 space stations were built with enhanced technology and a better design. Salyut 6 remained in orbit for four years and hosted several Soviet and international visitors. Over the four-year period, 28 astronauts visited the spacecraft and spent 2,117 manned days on it. Overall, the Salyut programme paved the way and helped develop and implement Mir, the next-generation space station.

All about Astronauts

An astronaut is a person who travels into outer space, but the term is commonly used for persons on US spacecrafts. The Chinese call them taikonauts or *yuhangyuans*, which in Chinese means 'space navigator'. Read on to know more about their brave journeys.

 ## Who can Become an Astronaut?

People who apply to become astronauts undergo a strict selection process. Experienced test and jet aircraft pilots, and those with advanced scientific, medical or engineering prowess are eligible. In the US, astronauts are classified into shuttle pilots and mission commanders, mission specialists and educator mission specialists.
In Russia, they have two categories: mission commanders, who are usually pilots, and flight engineers.

 ## How do Astronauts Prepare to Go into Space?

Astronauts undertake two to four years of rigorous physical and mental training and should be able to live in isolated and confined spaces for long periods. They undergo training in technical, safety, and survival techniques as well as handling emergencies. They are also trained in systems, robotics, spacecraft operations, space engineering activities, etc. Some of them working on the **International Space Station (ISS)** need to learn Russian to communicate with the Russian Mission Control Centre. The ISS was set up in low-Earth orbit mainly by the USA and Russia, with help and components from a multinational association.

▼ *Spacesuits protect astronauts from the hazards of being out in space. They are also known as Extravehicular Mobility Units*

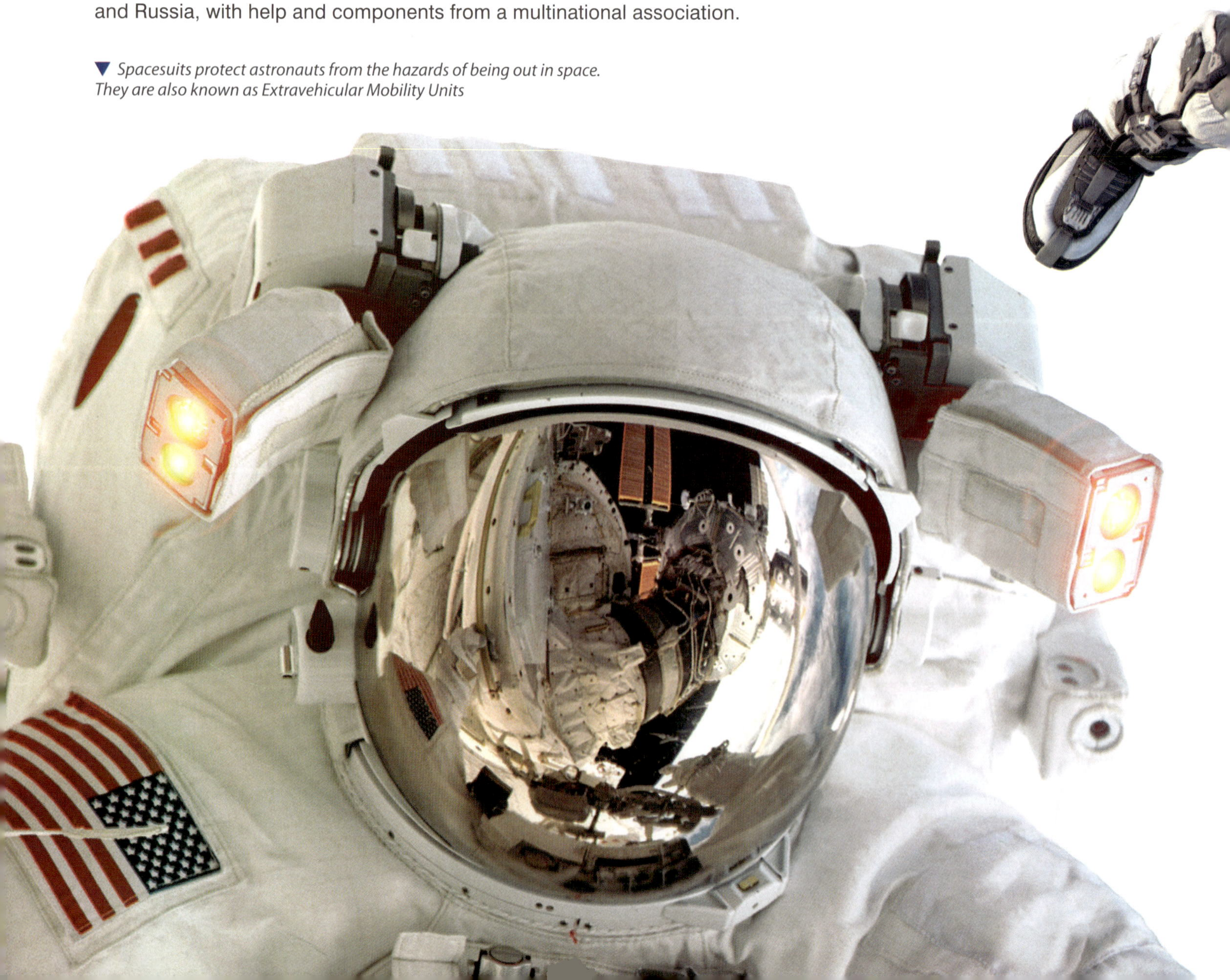

SPACE | MISSION EXPLORATION | 15

⭐ Simulations and Mock-ups

To prepare for space, astronauts often practice on life-sized models called 'mock-ups'. In the USA, the Space Vehicle Mock-up Facility serves this purpose.

At the facility, astronauts practice and learn to navigate themselves in a weightless condition called **microgravity** or zero gravity. The KC-135 (also called the Weightless Wonder or, humorously, the Vomit Comet) provides US astronauts with a zero-gravity environment for 20-25 seconds. Two other types of facilities help them practice moving large objects in space that have a tendency to float away, and practice spacewalks and rehearse on a full-sized model of a space vehicle, while underwater.

⭐ What do Astronauts Eat?

Earlier, astronauts had to eat unappetising edible cubes, freeze-dried powders and semi-liquids packaged in aluminium tubes. Freeze-dried foods were difficult to rehydrate and crumbs were dangerous since they could float off and destroy instruments on board. Since then, food eaten in space has improved considerably and astronauts today have a more appetising menu consisting of food items that can be prepared easily. Salt and pepper are only available in liquid forms since the powder form would pose a threat to both astronauts and the spacecraft.

▲ Astronauts float in space due to zero gravity, which leads to weightlessness

◄ A meal in space—astronauts eating floating tomatoes and hamburgers in the service module

⭐ Why do Astronauts Wear Spacesuits?

Spacesuits protect astronauts from harmful radiation and extreme temperatures experienced in space. They shield them against dangerous and fast-moving space dust particles that can injure them. The Primary Life Support Subsystem supplies oxygen for breathing and removes exhaled carbon dioxide. The visors protect the astronauts' eyes from harsh sunlight. A Liquid Cooling and Ventilation Garment keeps astronauts cool during a spacewalk.

👤 In Real Life

In space, flour tortillas are considered to be a better food choice than bread. This takes care of the problem of bread crumbs floating around. Meals and menus are planned in advance, and nutritionists ensure that the astronauts get their required daily intake of calories.

► An astronaut in a spacesuit

The First Humans in Space

The Soviet Union sent the first human beings to outer space. This was a huge milestone for them and for the entire space industry. Let us take a look at some of these pioneers.

⭐ Yuri Gagarin: First Man in Space

Yuri Gagarin (1934–1968), the son of a carpenter, initially studied at a trade school near Moscow. He later took up flying and graduated from the Soviet Air Force cadet school in 1957.

Gagarin made headlines on April 12, 1961, when he blasted into space aboard the Vostok 1 spacecraft at 9:07 am, Moscow time, orbited Earth at a speed of 27,400 kilometres per hour and reached a height of 301 kilometres. He spent 108 minutes in orbit before returning to Earth. Gagarin ejected from the vehicle and landed by parachute. He became a worldwide hero and was awarded the Order of Lenin amongst other recognitions and titles.

▲ At the Paris International Air Show (1965), Yuri Gagarin greets NASA's Gemini 4 astronauts Edward White II and James McDivitt

⭐ Valentina Tereshkova: First Woman in Space

After Gagarin's success, Soviet Chief Designer Sergey Korolyov wanted to send a woman to space. Earlier, it was assumed that the best candidates were military pilots, as they were accustomed to the stress of space flight, however, they were exclusively male. Since the Vostok spaceship was mostly automated, piloting was no longer a requirement, but parachuting skills were essential since Vostok cosmonauts were required to use and manoeuvre a parachute to help them land safely on Earth when they were ejected from the capsule.

For this reason, in 1962, Valentina Tereshkova was selected from among 400 female applicants. While Tereshkova had little formal education, she was an experienced and skilled parachutist. She became the first woman in space aboard the Vostok 6 on June 16, 1963. In three days, Tereshkova orbited Earth 48 times and successfully landed back on Earth on June 19. No other Russian woman went into space until 19 years later.

▲ Major of the Soviet Air Forces Valentina Tereshkova was the first woman in space

🎖 Incredible Individuals

When NASA opened up its astronaut selection process to women in 1976, Sally Ride was one of the 8,000 applicants. Women were being considered and selected as Mission Specialists for the first time. In June 1983, Ride blasted off into orbit on the Challenger orbiter, becoming the first American woman to go into space.

▲ Sally Ride was amongst the first six female astronauts to be recruited in the 1978 batch by NASA

The First Americans in Space

Let us now take a look at the incredible achievements of two interesting Americans—the first in space and the first to orbit Earth!

⭐ Alan Shepard: First American Astronaut in Space

Alan Shepard (1923–1998) was in the US Navy and had served in the Pacific in World War II. In 1951, he qualified as a test pilot and experimented, amongst other things, with high-altitude flying and in-flight fuelling systems. In 1959, he was selected as one of the original seven astronauts for NASA's Mercury mission.

Aboard the Freedom 7, Shepard became the first American to travel to space, doing a 15-minute **suborbital flight**, reaching a height of 185 kilometres. Shepard became a national hero. He also commanded the Apollo 14 flight in 1971 that landed on the Moon's Fra Mauro highlands. Amongst the many awards he received were the NASA Distinguished Service Medal and the Congressional Space Medal of Honor.

▲ *Alan Shepard, the first American in space*

⭐ John Glenn: First American to Orbit Earth

John Glenn (1921–2016) had an illustrious career in the US Navy, which he first joined in 1942. Besides flying for 59 missions in the South Pacific during World War II, he flew for 90 missions in the Korean War, and in the last few days shot down three MiGs (Soviet military fighter aircrafts). He became a US Naval test pilot in 1954 and did experiments which entailed flying F-8 fighter planes. In 1962, Glenn completed the first orbital flight (Mercury-Atlas 6) in his space capsule Friendship 7. Glenn successfully did three orbits and landed back on Earth 5 hours later. It was a feat which got him much recognition (earlier, in 1961, Gagarin had completed one single orbit).

In October 1998, he undertook another space journey as a **payload** specialist. The trip lasted for nine days on-board the Discovery space shuttle, where they did research on similarities in the natural ageing process and a human being's bodily response to zero gravity or weightlessness. The Presidential Medal of Freedom was awarded to Glenn in 2012.

▲ *John Glenn became the first American to orbit Earth aboard the Mercury 6 mission in 1962*

▲ *On his second space flight in 1998, John Glenn, at the age of 77, became the oldest person to travel to space*

The First Human Beings to Reach the Moon

On July 20, 1969, Neil Armstrong, Buzz Aldrin and Michael Collins created history by becoming the first astronauts to reach the Moon aboard the Apollo 11. Armstrong stepped onto the lunar surface—the first person to do so—with the famous words, "That's one small step for [a] man, one giant leap for mankind." Aldrin and Armstrong spent over two hours on the Moon collecting surface samples and clicking photographs. After spending 21 hours and 36 minutes on the Moon, they returned to Earth in a splashdown in the Pacific.

⭐ Neil Armstrong

Neil Armstrong (1930-2012) qualified as a pilot at 16 and served in the Korean War. After completing his degree in aeronautical engineering in 1955, he worked with NACA as a civilian research pilot, and later worked for NASA. He tested many supersonic fighters, including the X-15 rocket plane.

In 1966, as commander pilot of the Gemini 8, along with David Scott, he managed the first manual space docking with another unstaffed rocket. A glitch made the spacecraft go into an uncontrollable spin, but Armstrong recovered control and managed an emergency landing in the Pacific Ocean.

⭐ Edwin 'Buzz' Aldrin

Buzz Aldrin graduated from the US Military Academy in New York, became an air force pilot and served 66 combat missions in the Korean war. He did his PhD in **astronautics** from MIT. In 1963, he was the first person with a doctorate to be recruited by NASA.

His work on docking and rendezvous techniques for space vehicles led to the success of the Gemini and Apollo programmes and is still being used. Aldrin started underwater training to mimic spacewalking and completed five and a half hours on three spacewalks. He wrote several memoirs and books and was awarded the Presidential Medal of Freedom and the Congressional Gold Medal.

▲ *Commander of the Apollo 11 flight Neil Armstrong*

▲ *Lunar module (Eagle) pilot Buzz Aldrin*

🔍 In Real Life

All the crew members of Apollo 11 spent 21 days in isolation to prevent contamination by lunar microbes. After their successful return, the crew did a 21-nation tour and were hailed globally!

Extravehicular Activity or Spacewalks

Astronauts can't actually 'walk' in space due to negligible or zero gravity, instead they float. What exactly is a 'spacewalk' then? Whenever an astronaut gets out of a vehicle, while still in space, it is known as a spacewalk or an EVA i.e., **extravehicular activity**. In the early days of space exploration, it was a big deal for humans to 'walk' in space. Today, however, astronauts regularly undertake spacewalks, especially outside the ISS, to complete different tasks.

▲ *An astronaut performing an EVA*

Challenges on a Spacewalk

Spacewalks help astronauts conduct useful science experiments, test new equipment and repair satellites or the spacecraft. Pressurised spacesuits protect them and provide them oxygen to breathe and water to drink.

There are several risks involved when astronauts go on a spacewalk, including drowning in space—liquids don't flow due to zero gravity and a malfunction in the spacesuit, for example, can cause liquids to accumulate, which can prove dangerous for an astronaut; floating away into space; body fluids and blood boiling in case there is an accidental depressurisation of the spacesuit; and exhaustion.

Safety During Spacewalks

To ensure that astronauts and their tools don't float away in space, they usually use safety ropes or tethers attached to the spacecraft—this keeps them and their tools close to the vehicle. They also wear a **SAFER** (Simplified Aid for Extravehicular Activity Rescue), which has thruster jets, and can be used to return to the space station, just in case they get unstrapped from the tether.

Training for Spacewalks

Floating in space is like floating on water. On Earth, astronauts practice spacewalking underwater in a huge swimming pool. An underwater environment for training is very useful as it best simulates the weightlessness experienced during spacewalking. For every one hour of spacewalking, they train for seven hours in the pool. Another method is through **virtual reality** simulation. Virtual reality helps astronauts precisely simulate the circumstances of a spacewalk. They keep practicing and planning for months, even years, before their spacewalk.

⭐ Incredible Individuals

Russian astronaut Alexei Leonov was the first person to go on a spacewalk. He did this in March 1965 for a duration of 10 minutes. In June 1965, Ed White became the first American to do a spacewalk, during the Gemini 4 mission, and did so for 23 minutes.

▶ *L-R: Soviet cosmonaut Alexei Leonov and American astronaut Edward White*

Milestones in Space Exploration

The United States of America and Soviet Union were the key players in space exploration from 1957 till the end of Cold War in 1991. After the disintegration of USSR, Russia and US became collaborators on space missions and projects, for instance, the ISS. Major milestones in space aviation and exploration are listed below.

1957
October: The Soviet Union launched the first artificial satellite, Sputnik, into space. In November of the same year they sent the first living creature, a dog, into space aboard Sputnik 2.

1958
January: First satellite launched by USA—Explorer 1.

1960
August: Soviet Union's Sputnik 5 carried two dogs (Strelka and Belka)—the first living beings to survive a journey into space.

▲ The space capsule of Sputnik 5 in a museum

1961
April: Yuri Gagarin, a Russian cosmonaut, became the first human in space.

May: Alan Shepard became the first American to go into space.

1962
February: John Glenn became the first American to orbit Earth.

June: Russia sent the first woman into space—Valentina Tereshkova.

1965
March: Cosmonaut Alexei Leonov undertook the first spacewalk.

June: Ed White became the first American to undertake a spacewalk.

July: NASA's Mariner 4 transmitted the first photographs of Mars.

1966
February: Soviet Union's Luna 9 became the first spacecraft to land on the Moon.

June: Surveyor 1 became the first American spacecraft to land on the Moon.

▲ A photograph of Luna 9

1968
December: NASA launched Apollo 8; later, its crew members became the first men to orbit the Moon.

▲ The Apollo 8 crew in training

1969
July: The first humans landed on the Moon—Neil Armstrong and Buzz Aldrin.

1970
September: Soviet craft Luna 16 was launched and was the first automatic spacecraft to bring back soil samples from the Moon.

1971
April: Salyut 1, the first-ever space station was launched by the Russians.

November: The Mariner 9 probe became the first craft to orbit another planet—Mars.

▶ The Skylab space station prior to launch

1973
May: Skylab, the first American space station was launched—it was the first manned research lab in space.

1975
May: USA's Apollo 18 and the Soviet Soyuz 19 launched in the Apollo-Soyuz Test Project—the first joint US-Soviet space project.

1976
September: Water frost discovered on Mars by American probe Viking 2.

1977
August and September: The USA launched interplanetary probes Voyager 2 and then Voyager 1.

1979
March and August: Voyager 1 and 2 began sending images of Jupiter and its moons.

1981
April: The first space shuttle, Columbia was launched. In February 2003, on its 28th mission into space, minutes before it was to land, it broke apart, killing all 7 astronauts on board.

▲ Crew members of space shuttle Columbia died when it crumbled over Texas in February 2003

SPACE MISSION EXPLORATION

1986
January: Voyager 2 began transmitting images from Uranus.
February: The core section of the Soviet space station Mir was launched.

1990
August: NASA's Magellan, the first planetary spacecraft launched from the space shuttle, began mapping the surface of Venus using radar equipment. Also, the Hubble Space Telescope was deployed by space shuttle Discovery.

1992
May: NASA's space shuttle Endeavour began her maiden voyage.

▲ *Space shuttle Endeavour*

2000
February: USA's Near Earth Asteroid Rendezvous (NEAR) spacecraft began transmitting images of the asteroid Eros. A year later, NEAR landed on its surface.

1998
November: The first segment of the International Space Station (ISS), built in collaboration with the space agencies of USA, Russia, Europe, Japan and Canada, was launched.

1997
July: The Mars Pathfinder, an American robotic spacecraft, arrived on Mars and later began transmitting images.

1995
February: American astronaut Eileen Collins became the first female space shuttle pilot. In 1999 she became the space shuttle's first female commander.

▲ *Eileen Collins seated at the flight desk commander's station*

2001
April: American Dennis Tito paid the Russian space programme $2,00,00,000 to become the first tourist in space.

◀ *Dennis Tito (extreme left) was the first private citizen to visit the International Space Station*

2003
August: The Spitzer Telescope, the largest-diameter infrared telescope in space, was launched by NASA.

2005
July: A planned collision of a NASA spacecraft with a comet took place, to help study the building blocks of life on Earth.
Also, space shuttle Discovery (STS-114) was launched with seven astronauts aboard—it was USA's first 'Return to Flight' mission after the 2003 Columbia disaster.

2006
January: NASA's spacecraft Stardust returned to Earth with the first dust ever collected from a comet.

2007
August: NASA launched its Phoenix Mars Lander, which discovered chunks of ice on the planet.

2012
May: SpaceX launched its Dragon C2+ mission to send supplies to the International Space Station.
August: NASA's Voyager 1 probe, launched in 1977, entered interstellar space.

2010
March: NASA's MESSENGER (Mercury Surface, Space Environment, Geochemistry and Ranging mission) became the first spacecraft to orbit Mercury.
November: Curiosity, the biggest, most advanced robot ever sent to explore another planet, was launched by NASA. It landed on Mars in August 2012.

2010
December: SpaceX (Space Exploration Technologies Corporation), a private American aerospace company, launched a spacecraft into orbit and returned it safely to Earth. It became the first non-governmental organisation to do so.

2009
March: NASA launched the Kepler spacecraft to look for exoplanets.
June: NASA launched the Lunar Crater Observation and Sensing Satellite (LCROSS) to confirm the presence or absence of ice on the Moon. In November they discovered a significant amount of ice near the Moon's south pole.

2013
November: The Mars Orbiter Mission or Mangalyaan was launched successfully by the Department of Space–Indian Space Research Organisation (ISRO). At a cost of ₹4.5 billion, it is one of the cheapest interplanetary space missions ever. USA, Russia and Europe are the only others who have sent missions to Mars, and much to the credit of India, it succeeded in its first attempt.

2015
March: NASA's Dawn spacecraft became the first to orbit a dwarf planet, Ceres.
July: NASA's New Horizons, which had conducted a six-month-long study of Pluto and its moons, came closest to the planet.

2018
June: Japanese mission Hayabusa 2 arrived at the Ryugu asteroid. In September of the same year, it stationed the first rovers to operate on an asteroid. It will bring back asteroid samples to Earth in 2020.

2019
January: China's Chang'e-4 robotic spacecraft was the first to land successfully on the far side of the Moon (side facing away from Earth).
September: India's Chandrayaan-2 Moon lander, Vikram, made a hard landing on the lunar surface. It was targeted to make a soft landing on the Moon's south pole but ISRO lost communication with it moments before its landing.

The Apollo Programme (1963–1972)

The Apollo programme launched by NASA was an extensive space mission that went beyond making humans land on the Moon. In fact, it was aimed at establishing space technology, conducting scientific exploration and creating human potential to operate in the lunar environment. It also paved the way for exploring more distant places in the future.

▼ An astronaut on a lunar landing mission. Elements of this image were furnished by NASA

◀ Crew members of the Apollo 11 lunar landing mission. From left to right: Commander Neil A. Armstrong, Command Module Pilot Michael Collins, and Lunar Module Pilot Edwin E. Aldrin Jr

▲ The Apollo 11 mission badge

The Challenges

Landing humans on the Moon entailed taking-off from Earth, which rotates at over 1,600 kilometres per hour and going into orbit at over 28,000 kilometres per hour. It also involved picking up speed at the precise time to over 40,000 kilometres per hour and travelling to the Moon (approximately 3,86,243 kilometres away), which itself travels at about 3,200 kilometres per hour relative to Earth. Then the spacecraft had to orbit the Moon and drop a special landing vehicle on its surface. After it reached the Moon, the astronauts needed to do several experiments, take measurements, collect samples and leave instruments that would beam back important information to Earth. Finally, they needed to make the journey back home.

It was a gigantic task. A single expedition was insufficient to ensure success, and NASA needed to develop an extremely dependable system for undertaking this task repeatedly.

Exactly how this was to be achieved was not clear, but NASA, the Department of Defence, American universities and American industries had the basic scientific and technical knowledge required to say that it was possible. All these bodies with years of experience and knowledge came together from different fields, including military, civil aviation, etc. Engineering and management systems with extremely high levels of efficiency were devised to ensure dependability in complex machines.

Besides a Moon landing, Apollo expeditions aimed to develop technologies to achieve other space-related national goals—expanding the limits of technological achievements, implementing scientific studies and building human capacity to work on the Moon.

SPACE | MISSION EXPLORATION

▲ The Lunar Roving Vehicle

⭐ Overview

The first crewed Apollo flight was in 1967; the last was in 1972. The Apollo 11 flight of 1969 was the most famous—it landed the first humans on the Moon. The initial four Apollo flights tested the equipment for the programme, and six of the last seven flights reached the Moon—Apollos 11, 12, 14, 15, 16 and 17.

Apollos 7 and 9 orbited Earth to test the command and lunar modules, but they did not send back any Moon-related data. Missions 8 and 9 orbited the Moon to test different components and sent back photographs. Apollo 13 was unable to land on the Moon but managed to send back photographs. The six other flights which landed on the Moon sent back large amounts of scientific information and nearly 400 kilograms of Moon samples. They carried out various experiments involving oil mechanics, meteoroids, heat flow, magnetic fields, etc.

⭐ Spacecraft and Rockets Used

Apollo flights used two modules. One was a command module—a capsule with room for three astronauts—which flew them to the Moon and back to Earth. The second was the lunar module, used to land on the Moon, with a capacity of two astronauts.

The first few flights used a smaller rocket—the Saturn IB rocket, 22-storeys high, with two stages (parts). After the first section depleted its fuel, the second part would continue flying. The later flights used a more powerful rocket—the Saturn V. This had three stages, was much taller and was responsible for sending the Apollo vehicle to the Moon.

◀ Rockets used for Apollo missions

▲ The Apollo 13 mission badge

Mission Highlights of the Apollo Flights

APOLLOS 1, 4 AND 5

On January 27, 1967, the first planned manned flight, Apollo 204 (AS-204), later officially referred to as Apollo, caught fire during a pre-flight test, killing all three crew members—Virgil Grissom, Edward White and Roger Chafee. The fire took place in the command module.

Changes were made to the Apollo command modules thereafter. There were no Apollo flights numbered 2 or 3. The first Saturn V launch of AS-204 (November 1967) became Apollo number 4, and its last launch was numbered Apollo 5.

APOLLO 6 OR AS-502

Date: April 4, 1968

This was the second launch of a Saturn V and was a success, although two of the first-stage engines broke down and the third-stage engine did not reignite after reaching orbit.

APOLLO 7: THE FIRST CREWED APOLLO SPACE MISSION

Date: October 11–22, 1968
Mission: Tested the Command Service Module (CSM) with crew performance
Crew: Schirra, Eisele, Cunningham

Quick Facts

- Apollo 7 did the first live TV broadcast of Americans from space using a 4.5-pound video camera on-board.
- All three crew members developed a cold—an uncomfortable sensation, since it is very difficult to drain out the mucus which accumulates in the nose and head. On their return flight, the crew decided not to wear their spacesuit helmets or they would not be able to blow their noses and the pressure generated could burst their eardrums! They all took decongestant pills an hour before re-entry.

APOLLO 8: THE FIRST TO ORBIT THE MOON

Date: December 21–27, 1968
Crew: Borman, Lovell, Anders

Quick Facts

- Almost 69 hours into the flight, Apollo 8 passed behind the Moon and lost signal. The astronauts became the first humans to view the far side of the Moon!
- There were six worldwide live telecasts across five continents with good audio and video quality.
- On Christmas Eve, the crew read verses from the *Bible* and wished viewers a merry Christmas.

APOLLO 9: TESTED THE LUNAR MODULE

Date: March 3–13, 1969
Mission: Gained experience in rendezvous and docking; also tested the entire system, booster and command and service modules in Earth orbit
Crew: McDivitt, Scott, Schweickart

Quick Facts

- The first crewed throttling of an engine in space was conducted.

APOLLO 10: TESTED THE LUNAR MODULE AROUND THE MOON

Date: May 18–26, 1969
Crew: Cernan, Young, Stafford

Quick Facts

- A successful rehearsal of the first flight of a complete, crewed Apollo spacecraft to orbit the Moon was carried out, and except for the actual landing, it included all other aspects of a lunar landing.

APOLLO 11: FIRST HUMANS TO WALK ON THE MOON

Date: July 16–24, 1969
Crew: Armstrong, Aldrin, Collins

Quick Facts

- Approximately 530 million people watched Armstrong on television in the first colour TV transmission from Apollo 11 to Earth, when he stepped out on to the Moon's surface.
- President Richard Nixon spoke to the astronauts via a telephone link, and a celebratory plaque signed by him and the three crew members was left behind on the Moon's surface.
- Remembrance medallions with the names of the three Apollo 1 astronauts and two cosmonauts who died in accidents were placed on the lunar surface. Goodwill messages from 73 nations compiled in a silicon disk along with the names of leaders from Congress and NASA were also left behind.

APOLLO 12: THE SECOND CREWED LUNAR LANDING

Date: November 14–24, 1969

Mission: Landed on the Moon, put in place the Apollo Lunar Surface Experiments Package (ALSEP) and recovered parts of the Surveyor III spacecraft

ⓘ Quick Facts

- Scientists were specifically interested in the salvaged TV cable of Surveyor since some biological organisms were stuck inside and they wanted to find out if they had survived.

APOLLO 13: FARTHEST FROM EARTH

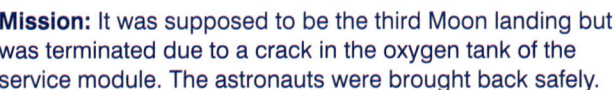

Date: April 11–17, 1970

Crew: Lovell, Swigert, Haise

Mission: It was supposed to be the third Moon landing but was terminated due to a crack in the oxygen tank of the service module. The astronauts were brought back safely.

ⓘ Quick Facts

- This was one of the famous Apollo flights, about which a movie titled *Apollo 13* was also made.
- It was called a 'successful failure' due to the experience they gathered from rescuing the crew members.
- Sufficient power supply was a problem. If the battery failed there would have been insufficient power to return to Earth. The electrical supply was switched off, and it became extremely cold.
- Water and food also had to be conserved. The crew started eating lesser, became dehydrated and lost weight.

APOLLO 14: EIGHTH CREWED FLIGHT TO THE MOON AND THE THIRD TO LAND ON IT

Date: January 31–February 9, 1971

Crew: Shepard, Mitchell, Roosa

Mission: Landed on the Moon mainly to explore the Fra Mauro region and carry out several other experiments

ⓘ Quick Facts

- Apollo 14 docked with the lunar module after six attempts.
- It was the first time that a lunar crew had spent 9 hours, 24 minutes in total on two separate spacewalks.
- Astronaut Alan Shepard established a new record of travelling the farthest distance on the Moon—approximately 2.74 kilometres.
- They collected almost 43 kilograms of rocks and soil, which were to be sent to 187 scientists in the USA and 14 other nations for studying and analysing.

APOLLO 15: FIRST USE OF LUNAR ROVER

Date: July 26–August 7, 1971

Crew: Scott, Irwin, Worden

Mission: Landed on the Moon and was the first of the Apollo 'J' missions, with a capacity to stay for a longer period on the Moon with more surface mobility. Amongst other objectives, the mission was to explore the Hadley-Apennine region; conduct lunar surface and orbital scientific experiments; and test and evaluate new equipment.

ⓘ New Records Set

- Heaviest payload in a lunar orbit (48,534 kilograms)
- Maximum distance travelled on the Moon's surface (28 kilometres)
- Most number of lunar spacewalks (3) and longest in terms of duration (18 hours, 37 minutes)
- Longest time in lunar orbit (145 hours)
- Longest manned lunar and Apollo expedition (295 hours)
- First satellite put in lunar orbit by a manned spacecraft
- First car to be driven on the Moon (crew travelled 28 kilometres in it)
- First deep-space and operational EVA

APOLLO 16: FIRST LANDING IN THE LUNAR HIGHLANDS

Date: April 16–27, 1972

Crew: Young, Duke, Mattingly

Mission: To study sample materials and surface features from a selected spot in the Descartes region; conduct surface experiments; and undertake in-flight experiments and photography from the lunar orbit

ⓘ Highlights

- The fourth ALSEP became operational after flights 12, 14 and 15.
- Small changes made to EVA equipment were tested and evaluated, e.g., longer seat belts on the Lunar Roving Vehicle, etc.

APOLLO 17: LAST HUMANS TO WALK ON THE MOON

Date: December 7–19, 1972

Crew: Cernan, Schmitt, Evans

Mission: Moon landing and study of surface features of Taurus-Littrow region, including sampling of older and younger rocks that had previously been brought back and studied on the Apollo 16 and Luna 20 missions

ⓘ Highlights

- Final mission in the J-type series—different from G and H series in terms of extended hardware capability, larger scientific payload capacity, and the use of the battery-operated Lunar Roving Vehicle (travelled 30.5 kilometres)

Jupiter and the Juno Mission

Jupiter is one of the most significant planets and is key to understanding the origins of our solar system. What is the reason for this and why did NASA launch the crucial Juno Mission?

★ Why Explore Jupiter?

Why explore and study Jupiter? After the Sun, Jupiter is the next most central object in the solar system and comprises hydrogen and helium—the same light gases which make up the Sun. Due to its humungous size and mass, and the fact that it was the first gas-giant planet to develop, it has played a significant role in the evolution of the other planets—including helping form their orbits—and other objects like asteroids and comets. By finding out the amount of water, and hence oxygen, on Jupiter, scientists can get a better idea of how the planet formed and how heavy elements—vital for life and the survival of rocky planets like Earth—were scattered across the system. Studying Jupiter also helps us understand the history of other giant planets that have been found.

★ Juno's Mission and Goals

On August 5, 2011, Juno blasted off into space from Cape Canaveral in Florida, USA. Juno was constructed by Lockheed Martin Corporation—a foremost American company whose main business is aerospace products—with some equipment sourced from across the globe. It was launched aboard the powerful Atlas V 551 rocket and entered Jupiter's orbit on July 4, 2016. It began collecting scientific data using instruments and probes below Jupiter's cloud cover. The mission had several tasks—to get more details about the origins of the planet, learn about its core or interior structure, its atmosphere and magnetosphere. It would also study Jupiter's **auroras**.

◀ After the Sun, Jupiter is the most dominant celestial object in the solar system

💡 Isn't It Amazing!

Jupiter's equatorial region has a huge concentration of harmful radiation which can destroy Juno's electronic systems. However, the explorer's close polar orbit helps avoid this danger zone. Juno will be exposed to radiation equivalent to 60 million dental x-rays in one year. It is also the most distant solar-powered explorer launched by human beings.

SPACE | MISSION EXPLORATION

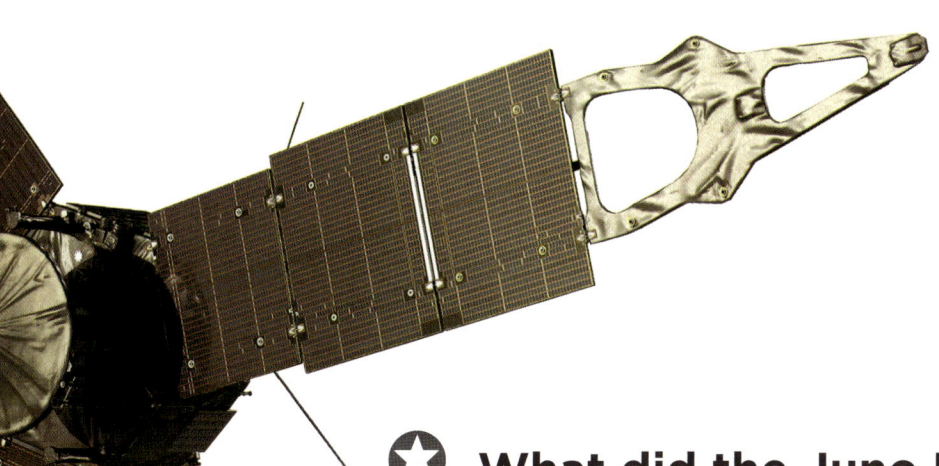

▲ *The Juno spacecraft near planet Jupiter*

⭐ What did the Juno Mission Accomplish?

The initial data collected from the mission reveals Jupiter to be an intricate, gigantic and blustery world characterised by deep storm systems which travel into the core of the planet, and a huge, uneven and bumpy magnetic field.

Juno's colour camera, JunoCam was used to show the planet's poles to the public, and also revealed polar cyclones the size of Earth that are tightly clustered and rubbing together.

The probe tested the thermal microwave radiation from the planet's atmosphere, from the top of its ammonia clouds and reaching deep down within its layers. The data revealed that Jupiter's belts and zones are enigmatic—the belt close to the equator juts all the way down; the belts and zones located near the other latitudes appear to grow into other structures. Atmospheric ammonia varies—it increases at the lower depths right up to a few hundred kilometres which is as far as their instrument can see.

◀ *The Atlas V-551 launch vehicle blasting off from the Cape Canaveral Air Force Station in Florida, carrying NASA's Juno planetary probe*

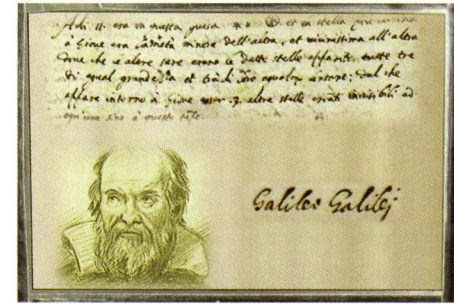

▶ *A memorial plate with some of Galileo Galilei's writings is aboard Juno*

👤 In Real Life

Accompanying the spacecraft on this 2.7-billion-kilometre journey are three aluminium LEGO figures of—astronomer Galileo, known for discovering Jupiter's four large moons; Juno, the Goddess after whom the mission is named; and her husband Jupiter, the Roman God.

▶ *The three mini LEGO statues flying in the Juno spacecraft—Galilei, Juno and Jupiter—are part of a joint educational programme of NASA and the LEGO Group to encourage children to discover science, technology, engineering and mathematics*

Exploring the Red Planet

Since the beginning of the space age, several Mars exploration missions have been undertaken by NASA and other international space agencies. The planet is a popular object of study. Let us find out why Mars has caught the attention of so many.

▶ *The OSIRIS instrument and filters on the European Space Agency's Rosetta spacecraft generated the first true-colour image of Mars when it did a fly-by of the planet in February 2007*

Why Explore Mars?

Mars is a **terrestrial planet** similar to Earth in climate and atmosphere. Like Earth, it has a complex **geology** and is the only other planet with signs of having supported microbial life. It will most likely be the first planet, other than Earth, that human beings inhabit. Important unanswered questions about the solar system can also be revealed by exploring Mars.

Mars Exploration Programme Mission

NASA's Mars Exploration Programme uses advanced technology to study the origins and early evolution of Mars, its geological and climatic processes, the biological potential for life on the planet and the possibility of sending humans for future explorations there.

Mars Exploration Rovers: Spirit and Opportunity

Mars explorations by NASA's twin rovers—Spirit and Opportunity (launched in 2003)—are the most famous. In January 2004, the two rovers reached opposite sides of Mars and began the most extensive exploration of the planet. The rovers traversed several kilometres, sending back more than 1,00,000 high-resolution photographs. They studied the chemical and physical composition of the Martian surface and found evidence of the presence of water in the past. Opportunity discovered rocks that seemed to be part of the shoreline of an old body of salty water.

The rovers were designed to last for 90 days but lasted much longer. Both braved harsh terrain, dust storms and climatic changes. By March 2010, Spirit stopped communicating with Earth.

Opportunity had travelled more than 45 kilometres, and by February 2018 had recorded its 5,000th **Martian day** (or sol). The rover stopped communication after June 10, 2018 and was finally declared 'dead' by NASA on February 14, 2019, after a successful and long innings of 15 years!

▼ *Twin rovers of the Mars Exploration Program—Spirit (left) and Opportunity (right)*

SPACE | MISSION EXPLORATION

⭐ Curiosity Mission to Mars

In November 2011, NASA's Mars Science Laboratory sent Curiosity—the largest and most advanced rover—to Mars. It reached in August 2012 and sought answers about whether or not Mars had suitable environmental conditions, in the past, to support microbes. With sophisticated scientific tools, Curiosity found chemical and mineral evidence to prove that it had a habitable environment, and has been exploring the Gale Crater and collecting and analysing rock, soil and air samples.

In Real Life

The Mars 2020 rover mission will carry MOXIE, an instrument to demonstrate how to generate oxygen from carbon dioxide contained in the Martian atmosphere.

▲ *A selfie taken by Curiosity rover at Rock Hall drilling site, on the Vera Rubin Ridge on Mars*

⭐ Salient Features of the Curiosity Rover

- Car-sized, with a 7-foot-long arm and 10 advanced science instruments
- Has tools including 17 cameras, a laser and a drill
- Uses a parachute and tethers for descending, which is a new and innovative landing method
- Able to mount knee-high obstacles
- Travels about 0.03 kilometres per hour
- Carries a special power system to generate electricity, enabling it to flexibly function in all conditions.

⭐ Significance of the Mars Science Laboratory (MSL) Mission

NASA's MSL mission to Mars, with its rover Curiosity as a part of its efforts to explore the planet with a robot, is a huge milestone for several reasons:

- Established the ability to put a large and heavy rover on the Martian surface
- Proved the ability to make a very precise landing within a 20-kilometre landing space
- Demonstrated long-range mobility on the planet to study varied environments and analyse samples found in different surroundings

▲ *Seen in the picture are all the components of NASA's Mars Science Laboratory (MSL) mission assembled together*

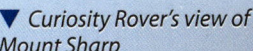

▼ *Curiosity Rover's view of Mount Sharp*

Challenges and Issues in Space Exploration

Though exciting and alluring, space exploration involves multiple challenges for the astronaut, such as an isolating environment, physical, psychological and emotional issues. Apart from that, it also poses the danger of overcrowding space with satellites, stations and space debris.

⭐ Impact of Space Travel on Human Beings

Human beings have evolved to live in the ideal environment provided by Earth. In space there are multiple adverse impacts. Astronauts often experience 'space sickness'—which includes vomiting, nausea and discomfort in the stomach. Usually, it lasts only for two or three days, until the brain adapts to the new environment, but may reoccur on Earth. Due to negligible gravity in space, everything floats, leading to loss of muscle mass, particularly in the calf and thigh. Astronauts on very long missions even lose a little heart muscle. Some weight-bearing bones in the body start to decay due to reduced usage. A daily exercise routine is, therefore, a must to prevent this. Studies have revealed that astronauts can lose, on an average, 1–2 per cent of bone mass per month! While these medical issues are not so problematic in space, they do adversely affect astronauts on their return to Earth.

Exposure to high levels of solar radiation can lead to serious health problems, including deadly tumours. On long missions, astronauts also need to deal with psychological problems that are a result of being confined to a small space with people of different backgrounds and temperaments.

⭐ Space Debris

After more than 60 years of space activities, our skies and space are full of man-made objects, including the ISS, the Hubble Telescope, communications satellites, space debris and rubble. Artificial material which is orbiting Earth but is not in use or not functional is known as space debris or space junk. A majority of space debris lies 160 to 2,000 kilometres above Earth.

Generated by deactivated or dead satellites, burnt-out rocket stages, lost tools and fragments of particles from object collisions, space debris poses a severe threat to the safety of spacecrafts and astronauts. The ISS and space shuttles with humans on board face this danger. Even a small speck of paint travelling at great speed is sufficient to damage space shuttle windows or kill astronauts. Hence, it is extremely important to keep track of space debris to avoid such incidents. In America, the Space Surveillance Network (SSN) operated by the US Air Force monitors and records space debris and informs NASA about any foreseeable collisions with satellites or the ISS.

▲ A piece of 'space junk' or debris—the propellant tank of a Delta 2 launch vehicle—landed near Georgetown, Texas, USA in 1996

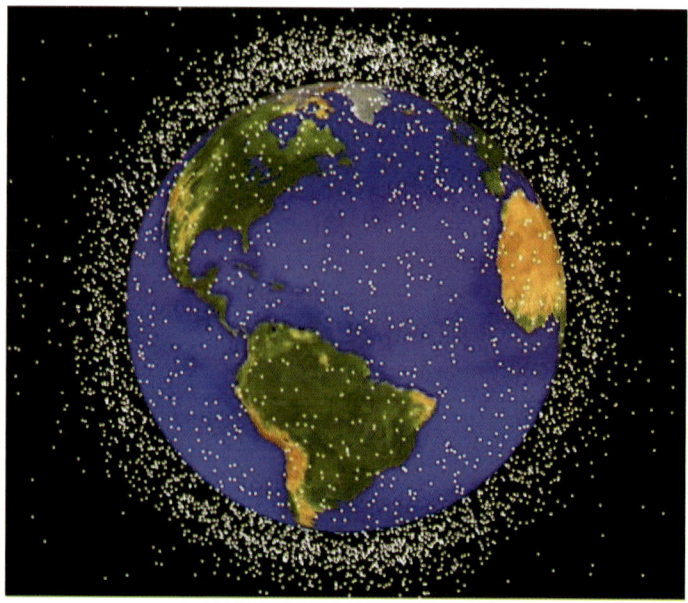
▲ The diagram shows orbital debris floating around in space

▲ *The International Space Station orbiting in outer space*

Damage Control

NASA has a set of guidelines and precautionary measures to deal with collisions with debris. When collision incidents are known beforehand, they move the station a little bit (Debris Avoidance Manoeuvre). If the tracking information is not too accurate, the crew is evacuated. Between 1998 and 2012, the ISS undertook 15 evasive manoeuvres. Since 2009, the crew has been evacuated thrice.

Isn't It Amazing!

Believe it or not but over 20,000 fragments of debris the size of a softball are circling Earth and travelling at speeds 10 times faster than a bullet! Additionally, 5,00,000 marble-sized bits and millions of other particles too tiny to track are floating in space.

The Outer Space Treaty

The Outer Space Treaty (OST) concluded in 1967, along with other United Nations treaties, sets forth guiding principles and a legal framework for space activities and is currently the only check for curbing and preventing use of military weapons in space. The OST refers to space as "the common heritage of mankind". The challenge is how to equally distribute the benefits of this common legacy amongst all nations.

▲ *A porthole of a space station*

Word Check

Aeronautics (also aeronautical/astronautical engineering): It is the science of designing, building, operating and testing aircrafts or vehicles that are used to travel in Earth's atmosphere or in outer space.

Aurora: It is an atmospheric phenomenon caused by the Sun, which results in dazzling and brilliant light shows in the sky. Auroras can happen not just on Earth, but also on other planets that have an atmosphere and magnetic field. They have been seen on Jupiter and Saturn.

Extravehicular activity (EVA): Whenever an astronaut gets out of a vehicle while still in space, it is known as an extravehicular activity or spacewalk.

Geodesy: It is the science of accurately measuring and understanding three fundamental properties of Earth: its geometric shape, its orientation in space, and its gravity field as well as the changes in these properties with time.

Geology: It is a science that deals with the study of Earth, rocks and other substances that form the Earth's surface.

International Space Station (ISS): It was set up in low-Earth orbit mainly by the USA and Russia, with help and components from a multinational association.

Interstellar space: It is the place where the Sun's constant flow of material and magnetic field stops affecting its surroundings.

Martian day: Also known as Sol, a Martian day is only 39 minutes and 35 seconds longer than an Earth day. There are 668 Martian days in a Martian year.

Meteorology: It is the scientific study of atmospheric phenomena, particularly of the troposphere and lower stratosphere. Meteorology entails the systematic study of weather and its causes, and provides the basis for weather forecasting.

Moonquake: It refers to seismic activity or lunar ground vibrations that can be measured by seismometers installed on the Moon's surface.

Microgravity: It is a measure of the degree to which an object in space is subjected to acceleration. It is more commonly used synonymously with zero gravity and weightlessness.

Payload: It is the load (passengers, astronauts, instruments, etc.) carried by a vehicle, like an aircraft, that is required for the purpose of the journey. It excludes what is required for its operation.

Rocket booster: One of the main parts of a space shuttle, it looks like a thin rocket and gives it a thrust to escape from Earth's gravity.

SAFER (Simplified Aid for Extravehicular Activity Rescue): It is a self-contained manoeuvring unit worn like a backpack. The system relies on small nitrogen-jet thrusters to let an astronaut move around in space. It serves the purpose of a 'life jacket' for astronauts while spacewalking and helps them return to the spacecraft in case they get untethered.

Space shuttle: It is a partially reusable rocket-launched vehicle that transports astronauts and cargo to and from spacecrafts that are orbiting in space. It is capable of landing on a runway when it comes back to Earth.

Suborbital flight: It is when the flight path (of a rocket, missile, etc.) is less than one complete orbit of Earth or any other celestial body.

Terrestrial planet: Also known as a rocky planet, it is a planet with a rocky surface primarily made up of silicate rocks or metals. In our solar system, the four planets closest to the Sun are referred to as terrestrial planets.

Virtual reality (VR): It is when computers are used to model and simulate real-life situations or events. It allows people to engage with an artificial 3D visual or sensory environment using interactive devices like headsets, goggles, gloves and bodysuits.